MY TONGUE IS
YOUR QUILL

STORIES AND ANECDOTES
HEARD FROM
RABBI M. MENDEL MAROSOW

Prepared for
his First Yahrzeit
Rosh Chodesh Shevat, 5779

By
Elchonon Lesches

Back Cover Photo Credit: Menachem Aron

TABLE OF CONTENTS

ACKNOWLEDGMENTS

With thanks to Bubby for the time she spent with me; Rabbi Levi Tenenbaum who spent many hours at Zaidy's farbrengens; my uncle, Rabbi Daniel Goldberg, for his help and expertise; the cousins who kept harassing me to "write something already about Zaidy"; and to the relatives who helped finance this project.

But mostly, to Zaidy, with whom I was fortunate —along with thousands of other bochurim—to spend many years of late nights, crammed in together around Zaidy, enveloped in the warmth of the true chassidishe farbrengen, reflecting, sighing, laughing, and resolving—while the world slept on around us— to make tomorrow a better day. Those farbrengens are irreplaceable.

THE LITTLE STORYTELLER

The steam locomotive made its appearance in Russia in the early 1830s. The country was most suited for railroads: Its long, flat stretches of land and broad steppes were the perfect backdrop for this new method of transport. Planning began for the building of Russia's first important railway that linked Moscow and St. Petersburg; when this was completed, the railroad splintered into thousands of tracks that crisscrossed the great country.

At first, people were wary of the shuddering metal dragon that belched steam as it roared across the railway tracks, wondering in disbelief if this contraption could really replace all their wagon drivers, but the Czarist government was very enthusiastic about this newest mode of transportation—particularly taking into consideration the extreme weather conditions. People now had a reliable method of transport, even in the worst blizzards. The railway would also help bring food grown in the South, home of the agricultural colonies, to the less fertile North.

Russia's railway became a gigantic network that linked all parts of the great country like never before. The general public became familiar with an entirely new world: ticket-masters, conductors, different classes of railroad cars, the loud whistle of the steam engine, train stations. People from all walks of life met on the Russian trains, spending hours–sometimes days or even weeks–in the company of all ethnicities. They gladly preferred the smooth clacking of the wheels across railroad tracks to the jarring bumps of the horse drawn wagon. The main advantage was that the system worked: anyone could buy a ticket, get on at the originating station and find themselves transported in relative comfort to their destination.

Zaidy often told and retold four incidents that occurred on these trains:

The first story was about his father, the famed Chassid Reb 'Chonye' (Elchonon) Marozow. After the Rebbe Rashab traveled to Rostov to escape the advancing German army, Reb Chonye decided to travel to the Rebbe for Tishrei. This was towards the end of World War I, after Germany had occupied wide swaths of White Russia and the Ukraine, forcing travelers to cross over areas controlled by warring factions. The Russians, humiliated by their severe defeat at the hands of the Germans, viewed all travelers with heightened suspicion and did not hesitate to accuse them of espionage—and shoot them on the spot. Typically, however hostile they were to the public, the soldiers were particularly brutal to Jews.

After toppling the Czar in 1917, the Bolsheviks fought against tattered remnants of the Czars' armies–each side trying to control the country. Bands of brigands rampaged around the country, massacring thousands of Jews in pogroms. The Rebbe Rashab had escaped by reaching the city of Orel, after which he moved to Rostov-on-Don.

(He remained there until his *histalkus*, after which his son, the Rebbe Rayatz, stayed there for another four years.)

It had been impossible for the Rebbe's *mazkir*, Reb Chonye, to leave Lubavitch with the Rebbe. His wife was expecting a child, and they had five children, who were mostly very young. So he stayed in Lubavitch. It was a dangerous time for a religious Jew to be outdoors at all, but Reb Chonye's yearning to see the Rebbe Rashab had reached a peak: he thought about it, spoke about it, and dreamed of seeing the Rebbe again. Finally, despite the danger, he set out to reach Rostov, accompanied by Rabbi Nochum Shmarya Sossonkin and another Chossid.

It was getting dark as the shrieking engine finally arrived, leaving quickly after passengers had filled its cars, picking up speed as it chugged toward Rostov. Within a short time, stone-faced soldiers boarded the train and took up positions in all the cars. "Passports! Documents!" they ordered. "Line up!"

The trio of Chassidim had no choice but to join the line of passengers. The soldiers found Rabbi Sossonkin's documents to be in order, and allowed him to travel further, but they did not accept Reb Chonye's documents, nor that of the other Chossid. "Make sure you both get off at the next station," they sneered. "Otherwise, it will give us the greatest pleasure to have you thrown off the speeding train to your deaths."

To say that Reb Chonye was devastated would be an understatement: *finally* he was so close to seeing his beloved Rebbe, only to have these soldiers stand in his path. But, realizing the severity of the situation, he got off at the next station; to continue would be sheer suicide. To his immense surprise, he realized that the third Chassid had no intention of disembarking—after all, he had invested money, time and effort into this journey, and no soldier would stop him. Reb Chonye tried to reason with the Chassid—to no avail.

Soon afterwards, as the train continued on its way, the soldiers checked the railway car and, finding the Chassid still on the train, threw open the doors and flung him out of the hurtling train to his death. Satisfied grins on their faces, they returned to their duties, leaving a horror-stricken Reb Shmaryahu to continue his journey alone.

Meanwhile, for Reb Chonye, getting off the train had exacerbated his already perilous situation. The station where he alighted was full of soldiers hostile to Jews, and suddenly one of them walked over to Reb Chonye and grabbed him. "Listen here, Jew," he said matter-of-factly. "I've just decided to shoot you. One less Jew."

"Wait!" Reb Chonye pleaded. "Grant me one wish before I die; let me say my prayers." Ironically, the majority of Russian soldiers in those days were religious Orthodox Christians, and the soldier agreed to let him pray. Reb Chonye *davened mincha* with the same fervor and emotion usually reserved for *Neilah* prayer at the end of Yom Kippur.

As he finished, and the soldier raised his gun, another soldier came by and pushed his arm away. "Leave him!" he spat. "What do you need that Jew for?" The soldier lowered his gun, let Reb Chonye go, and the shaken Chassid quickly found a train back home—to Lubavitch.

Meanwhile, having reached Rostov, Rabbi Sossonkin quickly requested an audience with the Rebbe Rashab, and told him the whole story, expressing his grief at the Chassid's death and voicing aloud his fears for Reb Chonye as well.

The Rebbe lowered his head for a few moments, momentarily in thought. "It is fine," he then said, "Chonye is already back at home!"

Zaidy heard both sides of the story years later, when Rabbi Sossonkin visited his father and they exchanged their recollections about this absolutely horrific train ride. Even these Chassidim of stature, who did not need additional proof about the greatness of the Rebbe Rashab, sat over-awed by the clear *ruach hakodesh* displayed by the Rebbe in this instance.

Many years later, when *Zaidy* was a *bochur* and the Marosow family was living in Leningrad, *Zaidy* was once riding the train when he became distracted, only realizing the train had reached his stop after it had already started pulling out of the station. He quickly jumped off the moving tramcar, landing on the station with a thud. Reb Chonye happened to be waiting for him at the station and, seeing *Zaidy* jump off the train, told him the following story:

"Over thirty years ago," he said, "when I was your age, the Rebbe Rashab sent me and some friends to stay for a while and learn under Reb Abba Person, a Chossid of the *Tzemach Tzedek* who lived in Konigsberg. Reb Abba had once been wealthy, but had lost most of his wealth, yet the Rebbe insisted he stay in his city. The Jews of the city greatly revered this elderly Chassid. They crowded his house at all hours of the day to ask him questions and advice; after they left, he stayed up all night learning *Chassidus*. Still, he spent much time *farbrenging* with us, sometimes reproaching us for not applying ourselves to the teachings of Chassidus.

"The Rebbe felt we had much to learn from Reb Abba. One day, as Reb Abba passed by the train station, he saw me doing what you just did—I was jumping off a moving railroad car. Reb Abba noticed this and called me over. He began rebuking me: 'Don't you remember what it says in *Gemora?*' he demanded. 'It says that when someone experiences a miracle, the merits he has accrued in Heaven are reduced—for having relied on a miracle.'

"'Chonye!' he said. 'How many *mitzvos* did you just lose? When you risk your life in such a way, do you know what harm you caused to your merits?'"

Another story that *Zaidy* sometimes told when the subject of *emunah* came up during his *farbrengens* occurred after the Holocaust. The railroad, still the most popular and busiest form of transportation, remained packed with people who filled its cars to capacity as they traveled across the country trying to find lost relatives and pick up the pieces of their shattered lives (usually without success).

After the cessation of war hostilities, persecution against Jews and Lubavitcher Chassidim in Russian resumed in earnest, but it was precisely during this period (1945-6) that most Lubavitcher Chassidim were able to escape the Soviet Union. This came about through a very interesting turn of events: after Germany invaded Russia, suddenly the Soviets became allies of the West—leading the British to push for reopened diplomatic relations between Poland and Russia. Stalin then promised to release tens of thousands of Polish citizens (including those interred in Soviet *gulags*) and allow them to return to Poland. By assuming the false identities of displaced Polish citizens, many Chabad families were finally able to escape the land of religious oppression.

Zaidy and his family were among the refugees who made it out of Russia. Due to an ailing infant, *Zaidy* and his wife were unable to travel with the bulk of the group—who had already been temporarily housed in DP camps in Poking, Germany—and they benefited instead from an incredible occurrence:

Allied forces, horrified at the near-apocalyptic scenes in the concentration camps, emptied some towns of their German citizens and turned over their homes to the war refugees—enabling them to enjoy a measure of comfort while they waited for visas. These fortunate families were able to move into a real house: suddenly they came face-to-face with comforts never seen before in a Chassidic Russian home: crystal chandeliers, couches, paintings, brocaded curtains!

Shortly after, on *yud beis Tammuz*, *Zaidy* decided to travel to the DP camp in Poking to join the large *farbrengen* where his fellow Chassidim would be celebrating the recent release of the Rebbe Rayatz from Soviet jail. He asked a fellow Chassid, Aryeh Gershoni, to accompany him on the train ride back to Poking.

Train schedules were unheard of. Passengers milled about patiently as they waited—sometimes for days on end—for the next train to pull into the station. As *Zaidy* came into the station, he and his friend noticed a cluster of people arguing, so they made their way across the platform to the group. Their gaunt features and prematurely aged expressions were the hallmarks of German Jews who had lived through the horrors of the Holocaust.

"I was fortunate to see Hashem's Hand on a daily basis," the first person was saying. "The Germans had herded us all into the ghetto. We spent hours and days wondering about our future—having already heard about the atrocities being committed by the Nazis—so that we lived in silence where there should have been sound, emptiness where there should have been activity.

One night, when I couldn't sleep, I found myself standing at the barbed wire fence that separated us from the world. Here and there patches of moonlight filtered through the heavy clouds. Suddenly, I almost cried out in alarm; a dark shape materialized before me. Just then, a bright sliver of the moon came out from behind the clouds and I saw a peasant woman standing at the fence, a finger on her lips. 'I can hide you until this is over,' she whispered. She then told me her address and disappeared.

"I walked around in a daze for the next day or two. Was

this a trap? Were the Germans behind this trick, to make a public example of me for trying to escape the ghetto? But the more I thought about it, the more nonsensical it sounded for the Germans to go to such lengths just to trick a Jew they despised. That night, after spending hours digging a trench under the fence, I crawled through it, made my way carefully to the address, and tapped on the window. The peasant woman opened the door and showed me a large pit she had dug under the floor of her home. 'You are safe here until the war is over,' she promised, 'I will throw down food for you every day.'

"After spending a night in the large pit, I became emboldened, and asked if she would agree to take more members of my family into her home. 'Yes,' she said, 'I live here alone and no one will be the wiser. Bring as many people as you can fit in there.'

"I made multiple trips over the next few days, smuggling various family members under the barbed wire fence and into the pit. We lived under the floorboards of her home until the end of the war; thanks to this Divine intervention I survived the war with many of my close family members!"

All the while he was speaking, the second person in the group was twitching impatiently, waiting for his chance to be heard. "How dare you!" he hissed, violent rage evident in his words. "Are you saying that you and your family were more saintly than my father—a *tzaddik* who sat all day wrapped in *tallis* and *tefillin* as he learned Torah? The accursed Nazis burst into our house, strangled him to death with the straps of his *tefillin*, ripped the *tefillin* off his head, put all our valuables in a sack, and tied the sack closed with the blood-soaked straps of his *tefillin!* Why were you allowed to survive while he suffered such an unjust death?"

The uneasy silence was quickly broken by the third person in the group. "And I will tell you that the Holocaust made me into a religious Jew!" he declared.

The group looked at him in shock, waiting for clarification.

"Growing up, I did not know that I was Jewish," he revealed. "My parents lived and acted like non-Jews and never mentioned a word about *Yiddishkeit* to me. Ironically, it was only when the Germans rounded us up together with all the Jews in our city in mass deportations to the concentration camps that my parents admitted we were Jews.

"The Nazis killed my parents as soon as we got to the camps, but I was sent to the other side—to work. The religious Jews in the camp befriended me; they began teaching me about our heritage and I learned how to read Hebrew. For the first time in my life, I was introduced to the concept of *davening* and of learning Torah. So, in my case, the war actually turned me into a practicing Jew."

Zaidy and his friend stood there quietly, absorbing everything being said, when the fourth in the group—the youngest by far, merely a teenager—started asking questions about the existence of Hashem, quoting all sorts of *sefarim* and secular literature he had found in libraries before the war. Gershoni, fascinated by the youngster, started answering his questions when the group suddenly heard the blast of the incoming train. The train shuddered into the station and some passengers disembarked. *Zaidy* and his friend quickly ran onto the train cars.

As soon as the train pulled out the station, the Jews on the train began walking through the cars, asking passengers "Amcho? Amcho (Are you from our Nation)?" This way, Jewish passengers were able to band together and stay apart from the accursed Germans riding the train.

Zaidy, Gershoni, and some other Chassidim were sitting together and talking, when they suddenly spied a youngster walking towards them, peering at the faces of the passengers as he went through the train cars. "There goes our young apikores," said Gershoni. As soon as he saw Zaidy's group, the teenager came over to them and said, "Trust me that I believe in Hashem!" he immediately exclaimed. "Living through the horrors of the war and trying to maintain my belief in Hashem leads to some questions; but not having any emunah at all leads to a lot more questions!"

"But this is what bothers me," the youngster asked Zaidy, hot tears streaming down his cheeks. "Let's say that what I saw during the war causes me to deny G-d's existence— why am I deserving of punishment if I cannot make peace with His existence?"

"From your statement," Gershoni interjected, "I am going to hazard a guess that you learned in cheder as a child."

The teenager bowed his head. "Yes, I did," he whispered.

"And I am also going to say that you learned in a chassidisher cheder," continued Gershoni.

"Yes," replied the teenager. He told them the name of the Chassidic court where he was raised and he then walked off, leaving the group immersed in thoughts.

At this point, without fail, whenever *Zaidy* recounted the end of this encounter on the train, he would start crying. "Just see the power of the *neshama*, the inherent value of *emunah* that Hashem has placed in each of our hearts," he would say. "Here you have a grown man who witnessed all the horrors of the Holocaust, who walked through fire and ashes, who saw the smoke rising from the death ovens, who saw the Angel of Death and lived—and yet, even after all his complaints against Heaven, after all his travails, only one thing disturbs his peace: *Why is he deserving of punishment for his lack in emunah.*"

(There was always a numbing silence after *Zaidy* finished this story. Chassidim did not usually tell stories about the Holocaust during *farbrengens*, preferring instead to gloss over their difficult travails and focus on the illuminating teachings of Chassidus. *Zaidy's* retelling of this incident was a departure from this custom; this encounter with a Jewish *neshama* had made such an impact that he continued living with its lessons throughout his life.)

Finally, the train story that *Zaidy* related most often, occurred a few years after the Rebbe Rayatz had assumed the mantle of leadership, and had moved from Rostov to Leningrad.

During World War I, when the Germans neared Lubavitch, *Zaidy's* family left Lubavitch and, a few years later, they moved again to Rostov, where his father resumed his duties as the attendant for the Rebbe Rayatz. After a short while, when *Zaidy* was eight, the Rebbe moved to Leningrad (Petersburg) and the Marosow family moved again.

In earlier years, religious Jews were not allowed to live in Leningrad. It was a beautiful city, but spiritually barren. Many war refugees made their way there during the war, but the city still lacked a structured yeshiva system. *Zaidy* and his brothers were little boys who needed to go to yeshiva, but their father was busy from morning to night in the Rebbe's house, so *Zaidy* and his younger brother, Herschel, were sent away from home—to learn in the Chassidic town of Nevel.

Arrangements were made with a young *melamed* in Nevel, Eliyahu Volovskin, to look after the boys during their stay. The teacher was young and newly married; he did not have children yet. The brothers learned by him, ate by him, and slept by him.

Zaidy reminisced often about those sweet days in *cheder*— the large room they learned in, with a long table in the center, around which the students clustered—and their nightly tradition of folding the table, placing some chairs together, and sleeping on the chairs. The class studied *chumash* all week, but, on Fridays and Shabbos, their Chassidic *melamed* did not teach; he sat his students down and related Chassidic stories.

In Elul, all the students and the Chassidim of the town traveled to the Rebbe in Leningrad. *Zaidy* and Herschel also went. Their happiness to return home was marred because Herschel felt feverish and very sick. Since they were little children—*Zaidy* was nine and Herschel was seven—they could not travel alone on the train, so an eighteen-year-old *bachur* from Yeshiva, Leibel Lipsker, accompanied them.

The trip from Nevel to Leningrad took twelve hours. Herschel looked so unwell that the conductor arranged a special place for him to rest. *Zaidy*, on the other hand, was unable to sit for so long, and he paced the train throughout the journey.

After several hours of traveling at night, when the first rays of dawn could be seen, Leibel called *Zaidy* over and said, "*Mendele*, you need to *daven*." He gave *Zaidy* a Siddur and showed him what to *daven*, but *Zaidy* finished *davening* too quickly for his liking. "You skipped some pages," he said.

It was possible. *Zaidy* believed him. "So I have to daven again?" he asked.

"I will show you where." The *bochur* pointed out certain sections and said, "You skipped here and here, say this over."

Zaidy was amazed. "How do you know what I skipped?" he asked.

"Some pages in the Siddur are illuminated and others are dark," he replied. "When you say the words, the letters become illuminated. The dark parts are the parts you skipped."

"But I don't see anything!

"You don't, but I do."

As a child, *Zaidy* believed him and he *davened* again

After *davening*, *Zaidy* continued wandering around from one compartment to another. As the train rattled along the tracks spanning the distance between Nevel and Leningrad, he found groups of Chassidim talking together in excitement about spending Tishrei with the Rebbe. Opening the door of a rail car, *Zaidy* found a compartment completely empty except for an eldery Jew who was sitting alone, a distinguished looking Chassid with a long white beard. *Zaidy* did not know that this distinguished personage was no less than the *rav* of

Nevel, Reb Meir Simcha Chein, and he beckoned to *Zaidy*. "Come, tell me something you learned in *cheder*," he encouraged the bewildered child.

Zaidy was more than happy to comply. Ever the storyteller, *Zaidy*—even as a young child—knew how to focus on a *chassidishe maaseh* and repeat it with all its details. And so, an unusual scene played itself out on the train traveling from Nevel to the Rebbe in Leningrad: the revered *rav* of Nevel listened in rapt attention as a youngster spun him a Chassidic tale:

"It all started in the times of the Alter Rebbe," *Zaidy* began, "when he had enlisted some of his most learned followers to travel around the country and secretly recruit outstanding young men to the growing ranks of Chassidus. These Chassidim would stop off in various cities, villages and towns, seek out the scholarly men studying in the synagogues, and impart select teachings of Chassidus, eventually drawing them to the Alter Rebbe.

"Now it once happened that these emissaries managed to attract the attention of an assiduous young scholar, a newlywed who was being supported by his father-in-law, and the infuriated father-in-law harnessed his horses and sped off to the Alter Rebbe to complain. 'Just look what has happened to my son-in-law ever since he started learning Chassidus,' he spluttered. 'Before your wretched followers came along, my son-in-law sat in the attic of our house studying Torah at all hours of the day and night; ever since your infernal meddling into his life, he hardly opens a *sefer* anymore. Instead, he just sits with a vacant look in his eyes and sits there thinking about something or the other.'

'Your son-in-law is not learning any less than he was before,' retorted the Alter Rebbe. "If anything, he is learning *more*. During all these years, when he was learning, he did so for a variety of external reasons—for the dog, for the cat, for your wife, for you, for his wife. You see, your son-in-law never learned too much up there in the attic, but every time he heard a creak on the attic steps, he would rush over to his *sefer* and bend over it, pretending to study. After some time, if no one entered the room, when he would go to the door to investigate the source of the noise, he would find it to be a cat or a dog. And, in the instance that you or your wife were coming into the room, he was already studying.'

'Now that he has been introduced to the teachings of Chassidus, he has no reason to pretend anymore,' concluded the Alter Rebbe. 'Whatever he learns is solely for the sake of Hashem and for no other reason.' The father-in-law bowed his head in acceptance and left the Rebbe's room."

Zaidy finished retelling the story and looked up to the *rav*. Reb Meir Simcha Chein nodded appreciatively. The train neared Leningrad and *Zaidy* put the incident out of his mind.

Upon their arrival, tragedy struck the family. *Zaidy's*

seven-year-old brother contracted a serious foot infection. He fell ill, thrashing in bed with fever as the infection worsened by the day, resulting in blood poisoning. He passed away shortly before Rosh Hashono; after that, *Zaidy's* distraught mother would not allow him to return to Nevel after Tishrei. His presence would gladden the hearts of those at home, distracting them from the missing child.

Winter came and went, budding foliage appeared on the trees, and soon Pesach had arrived. The weather improved; *Shovuos* was nearing. *Shovuos* meant scores of visiting *rabbonim* who would converge on Leningrad to spend the Yom Tov with the Rebbe Rayatz. The complex halachic questions that invariably arise in Jewish communities during Pesach prevented *rabbonim* from leaving their hometowns on Pesach; instead, they arrived for *Shovuos*.

One day, *Zaidy* came home to find his father sitting in animated discussion with one of his contemporaries, Reb Shaul Ber Zislin. Upon notic-

ing his son, Reb Chonye called him over and said, "Tell us the story you told the *rav* of Nevel when you met him on the train last Tishrei."

Mystified at the strange request, *Zaidy* began repeating the story he had told the *rav*, noticing that although his father was listening carefully, Reb Shoel Ber was shaking with silent laughter. Apparently, something about this story was very funny, but *Zaidy* could not figure out what it could be. Wasn't it a serious story? Intimidated by Rabbi Zislin's presence, he resolved to ask his father for an explanation once Reb Shoel Ber had left.

"It's very simple," Reb Chonye smiled broadly. "Every year, on *Shovuos*, the "old" Rebbetzin [Sterna Sarah, wife of the Rebbe Rashab] has a reception for the visiting *rabbonim*. It was there that the Rebbetzin related this very story, adding that she had heard the story from the revered *rav* of Nevel who had, in turn, heard it from—little Mendele!"

No one had an inkling that this little boy would grow up to become a storyteller *par excellence*, whose vivid, detailed descriptions of Chassidic life would inspire future generations.

MY TONGUE IS YOUR QUILL

'My composition of this Mizmor is for the King; my heart is moved to say good words, they flow from my tongue like the quill of an expert scribe (Tehillim, 45:2).'

"Just as a scribe needs to keep dipping his quill into ink to continue writing –

"So too, as long as my tongue can continue saying L'chayim, I will continue to farbreng about our Rebbeim and their Chassidim."

–Zaidy

IN HIS FATHER'S SHADOW

Zaidy's father, Reb Chonye, deserves a book of his own. A relative newcomer to Lubavitch, he later became known as the "Field Marshal" of Chassidus and personal secretary to the Rebbe Rashab and his son, the Rayatz. Stories, anecdotes, and Chassidic sayings about this fascinating Chassid abound—some of which are printed in the talks of the Rebbe Rayatz.

Zaidy never tired of talking about his illustrious father, peppering his *farbrengens* with stories about '*der tatte*':

After a fortuitous chain of events brought Reb Chonye to Lubavitch, he found new world open before him: young men studying *Chassidus* in depth, meditating with deep concentration as they davened for hours every day. And the *Maamorim!* The Rebbe Rashab was then in the middle of saying the famous *hemshech* of *Samach Tesamach* and never before had Reb Chonye heard such deep concepts. His interest deepened during Tishrei, when he experienced the *Yomim Tovim* for the first time in his life imbued with the spiritual aura based on the teachings of Chabad *Chassidus* that could not be found elsewhere.

After Tishrei, Reb Chonye felt torn between two worlds—he was supposed to be learning in the yeshiva of the Minsker *Godol* in Minsk, but he had now discovered a deeper level of *Yiddishkeit* in Lubavitch that attracted him. He stayed.

When the Rebbe Rashab established his new yeshiva, "*Tomchei T'mimim*," Reb Chonye became one of its first students. The Rebbe Rashab showed him great affection, and, at one point, even told him, "My door is always open for you. You can always ask whatever troubles you, and I will answer."

Convinced he could ask the Rebbe to explain in detail the entire *Tanya*, Reb Chonye tried on several occasions to ask the Rebbe to explain difficult passages in Chassidus, but, as soon as he entered the Rebbe's room, he became so overwhelmed by the Rebbe's presence that he could not speak. He envied the *chozrim* of the Rebbe who had no reservations about entering the Rebbe's room with a group of select students to review the *maamer* the Rebbe had said and ask for explanations. In contrast, Reb Chonye often told his children, "I could never open my mouth in the Rebbe's presence."

Many years later, during the famine triggered by the Soviet regime in the 1930's, *Zaidy*—then in his teens—met the person who had brought his father to Lubavitch. One day, as Reb Chonye was walking the streets of Leningrad, he saw a very old Jew begging for food. It was the same person who had offered him passage to Lubavitch! Now in his 90's, the Chassid had been forced by hunger and poverty to go begging on the streets. *Zaidy's* father took him home and cared for him.

Trying to repay his hosts' kindness somewhat, the elderly Chassid would describe to the Morosow children an incredible scene: *Tekios* by the *Tzemach Tzedek*! Having merited to spend Tishrei for *sixteen consecutive* (!) years in Lubavitch in the times of the *Tzemach Tzedek*, this Chassid was able to recall every detail of these special visits clearly, and would describe exactly how, every *Rosh Hashona*, the Rebbe's six sons would encircle him by standing in a specific order during *kriyas hatorah* and *tekios*. (When relating this story, Zaidy would add that, with the passage of time, he had forgotten the order.)

When the Rebbe Rayatz first approached Reb Chonye and proposed that he should begin serving as the private attendant and secretary of the Rebbe Rashab, he adamantly refused and no amount of convincing could change his mind. "But the previous attendant is no longer with us," said the Rayatz. "You will soon want to do it."

Within a short time, Reb Chonye was called into the Rebbe's room. He listened silently as the Rebbe Rashab began detailing the various responsibilities that would be incumbent on him and the different duties he would have to perform. "But Chassidim say that a secretary, privy to the Rebbe's doings, is not a Chassid," he said quietly.

The Rebbe thought for a moment. "True," he agreed, "but what can be done? Someone has to do it."

And thus, Reb Chonye became the Rebbe's *mazkir*. He rarely spoke to his family about the goings-on in the Rebbe's room, nor did he share with them any of the events that transpired with other Chassidim during *yechidus*—with the exception of three anecdotes. *Zaidy* sometimes related these events during his *farbrengens*, usually in the deep, quiet hours of the night:

"My father told us that being the Rebbe's *mazkir* involved a crushing workload and tremendous pressure. Yet, just having the ability to watch how the Rebbe recited Shema before retiring for the night outweighed all the difficulties.

"'I remember a *yechidus* time,' Reb Chonye told his children, 'when the *yechidus* line stretched out endlessly. Rich businessmen, struggling merchants, young firebrands, elderly Chassidim, and common folk stood patiently in line, waiting to be admitted into the Rebbe's chamber. I admitted them all, one after the other.

'As the last Chassid exited the Rebbe's room, I entered, as was my custom, to receive further instructions. 'You admitted too many people in tonight,' the Rebbe reproached me. 'You have wearied me.' As you can imagine, after hearing such words, I did not sleep a wink that night.

'The following night, mindful of the Rebbe's reproof, I studied the line carefully and, at a certain point, I deemed it necessary to cut the line. "The Rebbe will not be seeing anyone else tonight," I informed the remaining people. They were sorely disappointed. Relieved not to have taxed the Rebbe's health, I entered the Rebbe's room after the last *yechidus*, but he turned to me and asked for the names of those Chassidim I had not admitted. He listened carefully as I enumerated their names, interjecting when I mentioned a specific Chassid. "Ach!" he said. "*Him* you should have let in!" As you can imagine, I did not sleep *that* night either...."

'I could write a book of all the amazing miracles the Rebbe wrought, of the unbelievable wonders that he performed through *yechidus*. I remember one night when a particular Chassid arrived in Lubavitch and asked me to quickly arrange a *yechidus* for him, and then, for whatever reason, he started telling me the reason behind his urgency to see the Rebbe privately.

'A vicious anti-Semite had recently taken up residence directly across the house of this Chassid and he began abusing the Chassid and his family at every opportunity. He cursed and mocked them, even throwing heavy stones at the Chassid and his children, and the Chassid decided to ask the Rebbe for a *brocho* before the situation deteriorated even further.

'He had his *yechidus* shortly afterwards. The Rebbe Rashab listened quietly as the Chassid described his situation, but did not respond to his request, so the Chassid exited the room with a heavy heart. The Rebbe summoned me in, and immediately asked me to find out the name and mother's name of this anti-Semite, which I did. The Chassid then departed back home.

'The eldest child of that anti-Semite died that week. A few days later, his second son came home complaining loudly of a splitting headache and lay down to rest. He never got up again. When a third son died the following week, the gentile peasant realized this was no mere coincidence and attributed it—rightfully—to his religious neighbor.

'From then on, the gentile went out of his way to befriend the Chassid and to treat him respectfully, courteously wishing him a 'good morning,' without a trace of his former hostility. He was like a new person."

And then, on very rare occasion, *Zaidy* would relate the following incident:

"Although my father never repeated anything he saw or heard in the Rebbe's room during *yechidus*, one such *yechidus* made such an impression on him that he told us the details, incorporating it into the *chinuch* he gave us—the way he raised us to appreciate and respect the Rebbe. In deference, however, to the Chassid involved, he never divulged any names or particulars.

"One *yechidus* night, my father noticed a Chassid of great stature in line, someone who studied Chassidus assiduously and was well versed in many *maamorim*. Usually, when this Chassid entered *yechidus*, he spent the time asking the Rebbe questions on Chassidus—not on matters associated with his physical needs.

"This time, as well, when the Chassid entered, my father—who was in the room attending to other matters—heard the Chassid pose a question to the Rebbe on a *maamer* he had recently delivered.

"After a moment of silence, the Rebbe Rashab answered his question.

"The Chassid then asked the question again, restructuring the wording to approach the matter from a different angle. After a moment of silence, the Rebbe Rashab answered his question again.

"The Chassid then did the unbelievable: he asked the question once again, but rephrased the question to make it sound as though he was asking something else.

"At this point, the Rebbe Rashab eyed the Chassid carefully, sighed, and said, 'Vos anpest du? (Why are you needling me)?'

"Horrified, the Chassid took a step back and then ran right out of the Rebbe's room."

Zaidy told us that this incident shook his father to the core. 'After that," he told us, 'my father said he could never bring himself to even *look* at the face of this Chassid..."

Zaidy also told us that his father went into the business of manufacturing *talleisim* and even ran a factory that produced woolen *talleisim*. The Rebbe Rashab himself wore one of those *talleisim*.

Zaidy also mentioned his father innovated the way we string the *tzitzis*, changing the way the longest string of the *tzitzis* are wound around the other seven strands. Originally, the Chabad custom was to wind the loops along the top length of the *tzitzis* in the same manner as all other Chassidim, but Reb Chonye changed the process—so that instead of starting the second and third windings anew, he first completed the number of windings remaining from earlier sequences. (Since then, this has become the universal Chabad custom.)

Zaidy always made certain to clarify that his father's total devotion to the Rebbe Rashab naturally meant he would never dare to introduce such an innovation, without approval from the Rebbe first.

Before World War II, Warsaw was a major center of Jewish life in Poland. Her Jewish population of more than 350,000—the largest in both Poland and Europe—constituted about thirty percent of the city's total population, and Reb Chonye decided to travel to Warsaw on business, hoping to sell some of his *talleisim* there. When he returned to Lubavitch, the Rebbe Rashab summoned for him. "Tell me," said the Rebbe. "Did you visit any of the Rebbeim who live in Poland?"

Reb Chonye felt taken aback by the question; such an idea had never entered his mind. What business did he have in other Chassidic courts? "Next time you go," continued the Rebbe, "make sure to do so."

The *mazkir* left the room with mixed emotions: what did the Rebbe expect him to do in other Chassidic circles? Would not such a visit interfere with his complete devotion to the Rebbe? Despite his misgivings, next time he visited Warsaw, he remembered the Rebbe's words and thought long and hard how to fulfill this peculiar instruction. As *mazkir* and confidante of the Rebbe, if felt instinctively wrong to go and offer a formal '*Sholom*' handshake greeting. Instead, he opted to attend a *tisch*, when Polish Chassidim gather around their Rebbe for a Shabbos meal.

Zaidy never heard from his father exactly which Chassidic court he visited in Poland, nor the name of the Rebbe leading the *tisch*. All his father said was that he watched attentively how that Rebbe recited *Kiddush*, cut *challa*, ate his food, distributed *shirayim*—leftover morsels from the Rebbe's plate—and how he delivered brief Torah insights at the meal. In many respects, it differed markedly from the manner and comportment of the Rebbe Rashab.

Later, after returning to Lubavitch, Reb Chonye waited in vain for the Rebbe Rashab to ask him whether he had visited a Rebbe in Poland. When the subject was never mentioned again, he remarked privately about the outcome of this unusual directive. "I gained much from this visit," he said. "Everything I saw there was different from the way our Rebbe conducts himself; this visit helped me better understand the unique character of Chabad and its *Rebbeim*."

On the subject of unique character, *Zaidy* oftentimes

repeated an analogy he heard from his father to explain the unique character of one who has studied in *Tomchei Tmimim.* "After my wedding," related Reb Chonye, "I went with my wife to buy furniture. As we entered the ground floor, the salesman showed us the pieces on display: low-priced, simply designed furniture. Similar pieces with imperfections were slightly discounted in an adjoining room. When we went up to the second floor, we were shown expensive furniture of an entirely different class. Here too, in an adjoining room, we found similar furniture at hugely discounted prices.

"Can you explain the discrepancy to me?" Reb Chonye asked of the salesman. "The damaged furniture on the lower floor is slightly reduced, while these are greatly reduced?"

"The furniture on this floor is fashioned out of a completely different type of wood," replied the salesman with a superior smile. Seeing Reb Chonye's confusion, the salesman continued by explaining that the furniture upstairs was of such superior wood and craftsmanship that even a minor nick drastically slashed its worth. Even so, it remained far more valuable than the unblemished furniture pieces being displayed downstairs.

"This is the unique quality of a *Tomim*," *Zaidy's* father often explained at *farbrengen.* "*Tomchei Tmimim* enhances his essential qualities to such an extent that he is 'made of a different cut!' Although, at that level, every imperfection—however insignificant—becomes magnified, still, even with those imperfections, his essential qualities remains on a far higher level than someone who has not learned in Tomchei Tmimim."

Although *Zaidy* did not actually ever see the Rebbe Rashab—the Rebbe had departed Lubavitch for Rostov four years before *Zaidy* was born—the influence of the Rebbe Rashab had an impactful imprint on the Marasow home, especially since *Zaidy's* father had served as the Rebbe's *mazkir.*

There was one particular story *Zaidy* loved repeating. After the Rebbe Rashab escaped to Rostov, the deteriorating security situation caused by the war made it incredibly difficult for Chassidim to communicate with the Rebbe. Furthermore, in an effort to bolster his family's safety, the Rebbe canceled all private *yechidus* meetings.

During that time, the patriarch of the Itkin family became extremely ill. His family consulted with the best doctors in the field; to their consternation, all the doctors were in agreement that he could only expect to live if he underwent a complicated operation.

The family found themselves in a real quandary: they did not want to agree to such a risky operation with the Rebbe's express consent and blessing, but the Rebbe was not seeing anyone!

A member of the family traveled to Rostov and tried pleading his case with the Rebbe's attendant, hoping an exception could be made for this life-and-death situation. "Nothing can be done," the *mazkir* shook his head. "The Rebbe is adamant about not seeing anyone privately for *yechidus.* City officials are monitoring his every move."

Seeing the crestfallen expression of the petitioner, the *mazkir* relented somewhat. "I'll give you a suggestion," he said, "but you cannot say I gave you the idea. At some point, the Rebbe will have to use the washroom. Stand by the sink outside the washroom and use your ingenuity to find a way to communicate with the Rebbe without speaking to him..."

The petitioner immediately sat down and wrote his request on a palm-sized paper. Then he took up position near the sink outside the washroom and began waiting.

Hours passed. Suddenly the door to the Rebbe's room opened and the Rebbe Rashab came down the hallway. He did not even spare a glance at the Chassid near the sink, pressed against the wall, his arm held up to eye level, a piece of paper in his open palm.

A few minutes later, when the Rebbe used the sink to wash his hands, he started saying the *Asher Yotzar* blessing while simultaneously reading the paper in the Chassid's palm. The Rebbe ended the blessing out loud by saying, "'Blessed are You who heals all flesh and perform wonders'—*an operation is not needed.*"

The Rebbe's blessing thus secured, the Chassid returned to the home of the Itkins and told them what had transpired. They canceled the surgery, the Chassid recovered and went on to live a regular life.

THE WAY WE EAT AND DRINK

"Then Yakov gave Eisav bread and some lentil stew,

he ate,

he drank,

he got up,

he left (Bereishis 25:34)."

Why do we need all these descriptions? All we need to know is that Yakov gave Eisav some food. Or is there a deeper instruction here?

The Torah is teaching us an important lesson: a person can be a religious Jew, and not even realize that his day-to-day behavior is more befitting to Eisav than it is to Yakov.

The way we eat should be the way Chassidus teaches us,

How we drink should be the way Chassidus teaches us,

The way we get up should be the way Chassidus teaches us,

Our comportment and the way we walk on the street should be the way Chassidus teaches us."

—Zaidy

ENCOUNTERS

Not long after *Zaidy* was born, the family moved to the city of Krementchug, closer to the Rebbe in Rostov. While there, Reb Chonye was employed as the manager of a tobacco factory belonging to a wealthy Chabad Chassid. Although Reb Chonye worked successfully at his position, he once had a severe falling out with his employer, which caused his abrupt dismissal. After agreeing to sell a certain item to a customer at its wholesale price, the value of that commodity rose sharply, so that, when the customer came for his merchandise, the owner expected to sell the item at the current, higher price. But *Zaydie's* father felt that honesty dictated it be sold at the original price, and he did so, causing him to lose his job.

The Marosow family then moved to Yekaterinoslav (Dnepropetrovsk)-even closer to Rostov. There they stayed for a while at the home of Rabbi Levik and Rebbetzin Chana Schneersohn—the Rebbe's parents. While there, Reb Chonye studied *Chassidus* together with Reb Leivik, until they were able to afford their own home in the city.

Within a few years, after the Rebbe Rayatz had moved back to Leningrad, Reb Chonye took his family and moved to Leningrad as well—to serve as the Rebbe's *mazkir*. The Marosow family lived in close proximity to the Rebbe—on the same floor of the same residential building—and *Zaidy* encountered many great people during those years.

No matter whom he met, nothing could replace what *Zaidy* saw and experienced in the time their family lived so close to the Rebbe Rayatz. His sisters became childhood friends of the Rebbe's daughters. His mother—back then, she was called *Tante Brocho* by others—became close to the Rebbe's family members.

Decades later, when any of his grandchildren would eat the Shabbos day meal, if anyone tried to sit while reciting *Kiddush, Zaidy* would get very upset. "We lived across the hall from the Rebbe Rayatz," he would tell us. "When the door of the Rebbe's apartment was left open, we could see directly into the dining room and I could see the Rebbe Rayatz standing while he made *Kiddush. Nu,* if the Rebbe would stand—why are you sitting?"

Years earlier, before *Zaidy* was even born, his two older sisters, Rochel Leah and Sherel, had become very friendly with the three daughters of the Rebbe Rayatz, and often visited at their home to play with them.

At that time, the Rayatz's home was attached to the home of his father. Once, the Marosow girls started playing "blind man's bluff" with the

Rebbe's daughters. Each child had a turn to cover their eyes with a cloth and try feeling their way around the room, whispering and giggling as they tried to catch each other, while everyone ran around trying to escape.

When it was Rochel Leah's turn to wear the blindfold, she started wandering around the room, feeling around with her hands, when she suddenly caught someone. She pulled the cloth off her eyes to find that—she had "caught" the Rayatz! He had just then come into the room! Rochel Leah was horrified. She became very agitated as she tried to apologize, but the Rayatz calmed her fears. "You caught me," he said, "so now it's my turn to be 'it!'" He placed the cloth over his eyes and continued playing the game, trying to find the children as they scampered back into their hiding places.

After a few minutes passed, the door to the room opened, and Reb Chonye came in—almost passing out in shock. The Rebbe's son was playing a game with children! "Your father is calling you," he remarked to the Rayatz.

The Rayatz pulled off the blindfold and excused himself to the girls. "I was searching for my children," he said, "but now my father is looking for *his* child!"

Zaidy himself had a similar experience when he was still a young child—around six or seven years old. It was after the passing of the Rebbe Rashab and his son, the Rayatz, had assumed the mantle of leadership. The Marosow family was living then in Rostov, and *Zaidy* would sometimes scamper over and run around the apartment of the Rebbe Rayatz. The biggest room in the apartment was *der yechidus tzimmer*— where Chassidim met the Rebbe in a private audience—and *Zaidy* particularly liked running around that spacious room.

Sometimes, the Rebbe Rayatz was sitting at his desk, learning from a *sefer* or busy with his voluminous correspondence, while *Zaidy* would be running around the room making noise...

One day, when *Zaidy* ran into the unlocked *yechidus* room, he found the Rebbe Rayatz sitting on a chair in the middle of the room, lost in thought. He beckoned toward *Zaidy* and asked, "Where is your *Yetzer Tov?*"

Zaidy pointed to his heart.

"Your *Yetzer Hora?*"

Zaidy pointed again to his heart.

"And where is your *neshama?*"

Nonplussed, *Zaidy* pointed to his forehead, thinking that, perhaps, the soul resides in the brain.

"And what do you have inside your *neshama?*"

Zaidy was stuck; he had no idea what to answer.

"You should know," said the Rayatz, "that inside your *neshama* is another little 'neshama'le.'

Zaidy ran right out of the room, only to find a group of Yeshiva students standing in wait for him outside in the hallway. There were a pair of glass doors in the hallway; they had seen *Zaidy* go in and out from the Rebbe and were waiting to get a full report of what had happened in the *yechidus* room.

As soon as *Zaidy* came within their reach, one of the students picked him up and placed him on his lap. "Did they Rebbe speak to you while you were in there?" they asked.

"Yes."

"What did the Rebbe tell you?"

Zaidy repeated the entire conversation, not expecting the furor that immediately broke out amongst the students. "The Rebbe was referring to *yechida*, the innermost recesses of the Divine soul, as the 'little *neshama'le*,'" said one.

"Not at all," retorted the other. "He was referring to the *nitzutz haBoreh*—the Divine spark that resides in us all and gives us life."

The boy forgotten, they lowered *Zaidy* to the floor and let him run off. The sounds of their intense arguments would continue ringing in his ears for another ninety years.

Another giant in Jewish history *Zaidy* often spoke about was Rabbi Yosef Rosin—the Rogatchover *gaon*—the foremost Talmudical genius of his time. His photographic memory and legendary ability to connect seemingly un-related Torah sources to each other changed the face of Torah learning.

During World War I, the Rogatchover moved from his home in Dvinsk to Leningrad (and moved back to Dvinsk a few years later). Due to this move, it came about that the Rogatchover and the Rebbe Rayatz both resided in Leningrad until the beginning of 1925. *Zaidy* was a child at the time. He very often repeated an interaction he had with the *gaon* during that period, and also related other stories about the *gaon* that he later heard from other Chassidim living then in Leningrad.

Zaidy sometimes told two short anecdotes about the razor sharp responses of the Rogatchover. Once, a group of scholars were sitting in the dining room of the *gaon*, talking in learning, when the discussion turned to the order of precedence for making *brochos* over the food spread on the table before them.

"We can deduce the answer from a *possuk*," someone said. "It says, 'And Avraham moved from there to the mountain; he pitched his tent and the city of Ai was to the fore (*Breishis*, 12:8.)' From here we see that *Ai*, an egg (in *Yiddish* an egg is called an *Ai*), has precedence before the other foods. So we should eat the eggs first."

The *gaon* became extremely irate at this attempt to a convolute the simple meaning of a *possuk* in order to derive a *halacha*. "If so," he said with his trademark causticity, "I see I am sitting among a company of mockers (*moshav leitzim*)!" And he left the room.

Another incident occurred in a similar setting, with a group of learned scholars sitting around a set table, conversing in Torah with the Rogatchover. When it came time to *bentch*, a discussion started about whom to honor with *bentching*. "One of the people here is named Mordechai," said one of the guests. "Since we say '*Boruch* Mordechai' on Purim, that indicates that a 'Mordechai' should *bentch* (Boruch)."

The *gaon* was well pleased with this innovation and gestured for the said Mordechai to lead the *bentching*.

"In my youth," said *Zaidy*, "I *davened* in the Chassidic shul of Leningrad where the Rogatchover *davened*. In deference to his saintliness and scholarship, the *shul* allocated a special seat against the eastern wall of the *shul* for the Rogatchover. The *gaon* was of diminutive stature, so that even when he stood at full height in his place behind the *chazzan's* lectern, the lectern still concealed him. I would sit all the way in the back of the *shul*.

"There was also a *minyan* of misnagdim in the city, but one day, it seems their *shul* was closed, and a misnagid came over to the Chassidic *shul* for *shacharis*. Now, misnagdim have the custom to begin *shacharis* by having someone recite the Morning Blessings aloud, and, in this case, this man had arrived in *shul* late, yet completely ignored the ongoing *minyan* and began to recite the Morning Blessings out loud, forcing everyone to stop and answer *amen*.

"As soon he heard the misnagid, the Rogatchover shot out from his seat behind the *chazzan's* lectern and ran towards me in the back of the *shul*. His eyes met mine as he smiled broadly and said, '*Yingele, yingele*, look how a misnagid behaves ...' and he laughed."

Zaidy never tired of telling this story. It impressed him to no end that the *gaon*, blessed with such masterful recall of his surroundings, knew there was a little child *davening* in the back of the *shul*—a child he could not even see! It impressed him even more to see the *gaon's* reaction to the misnagid!

Throughout his life, despite not being an official chassid, the Rogatchover maintained very close connections to

Chabad Chassidim and their Rebbeim (he strongly supported the decision to appoint the young Rayatz as the new Rebbe). His name often comes up during *farbrengens*, with stories told about his self-sacrifice and dedication to Torah despite the pressures of the Russian government, yet *Zaidy* always liked to tell over a specific encounter between the *gaon* and emissaries of the Rebbe Rayatz.

"The *gaon* severely neglected his physical needs," *Zaidy* related. (In fact, the first time *Zaidy* saw the Rogatchover, he thought that this was a simple, unkempt person—until his father set him straight.) All he cared about were the *seforim* strewn across the room. His poor wife had a difficult time getting him to eat anything, to keep body and soul together. Sometimes, she would come into the room with a plate and he would look at the plate with an expression of incomprehension—he was still in a different world, elevated to a different plane of existence. After a few minutes of pleading, he would notice the food and eat a few bites. This was his "meal."

"Due to this situation, the Rebbetzin was fiercely watchful of the short timeframe when the *gaon* ate his so-called "meals," and did not brook any sort of interruption. One morning, the Rebbe Rayatz—who was much younger than the *gaon*—needed to consult with the Rogatchover about something, so he sent two Chassidim to call the *gaon*. When they arrived at the *gaon's* house, his wife was not at all pleased to see them. 'My husband is *davening* and then he still has to eat something,' she said. 'Please come back later.'

"The Chassidim, cognizant the Rebbe was waiting for the *gaon*, waited but a short time before they returned. This time, they found the *gaon* sitting at a set table, having just started to eat. As soon as he saw them, he reached over and took a *siddur* to start *bentching*, so he could leave with them back to the Rebbe. His wife started to protest, but he turned to her and flatly said, 'It is not befitting for me to delay them any longer; *the Nassi is summoning me!*'

He then left his home and accompanied the Chassidim to the residence of the Rebbe Rayatz.

Zaidy always told this story in connection to the fact that the Rebbe refers to his father-in-law with the title "*Nassi*." This title is not found in earlier writings of Chabad Rebbeim, nor was it part of the vernacular of Chabad Chassidim back in Russia and Europe when they referred to the Rebbeim. As such, hearing the Rogatchover—a towering genius in a generation of Torah giants—use this appellation in reference to the much younger Rebbe Rayatz made an everlasting impression.

While on the subject of stories about the Rogatchover *gaon*, *Zaidy* often related a tragic episode that occurred in 1924, while the Rebbe Rayatz still lived in Rostov. The Rebbe had given instructions for the branch of Tomchei Tmimim operating in Charkov to move to Rostov—thus enabling the *bochurim* to be in close proximity to the Rebbe and hear his *maamorim*.

After the yeshiva relocated to Rostov, members of the faculty complained to the Rebbe about Hirshel, an eighteen-year-old student, a newcomer to Lubavitch. For several months, Hirshel studied very diligently at the yeshiva and, although his fellow students apparently did not realize Hirshel's special qualities, the faculty realized that the boy was overextending himself with his studies.

Unfortunately, a few months later, Hirshel became afflicted with an unusual form of hepatitis, which prevented him from functioning normally. He began sleeping an abnormal number of hours—at first nine hours a night, then ten, then longer and longer. He had to be hospitalized.

The Rebbe Rayatz was deeply concerned about the boy and often asked for updates about his condition. Trying, no doubt, to avoid causing the Rebbe heartache, Reb Chatche Feigin would report that Hirshel was improving. To this the Rebbe replied, "*Halevai* [if only this were true]!"

Tragically, Hirshel passed away, and suddenly everyone realized how the Rebbe alone had understood the severity of this illness. They were further shocked when the Rebbe announced his intention that he would attend the funeral and even travel to the cemetery. Years earlier, when several students in Rostov had perished in a typhus epidemic, the Rebbe participated in their funerals only by coming out when their hearse passed his home—or sometimes not at all. It was unheard of for the Rebbe to go to the cemetery for a student's funeral! Especially a newcomer to Chabad!

True to his word, the Rebbe traveled to the cemetery. As the coffin was brought to the grave, the Rebbe assisted in helping carry the *aron* and, throughout the burial, gazed intently into the grave. That Shabbos, the Rebbe delivered a *maamor* starting with the verse *Im ruach hamoshel* (published in Sefer Hamaamorim 5684), which explains how the greatest Jews suffer for the sins of their generation. Only then did everyone realize that Hirshel, apparently, possessed a soul of exalted level!

Seeing the level of interest the Rebbe displayed for this youngster, the local *chevra kadisha* revealed a problem they noticed during the *taharah* process: after Hirshel had died, the hospital, apparently, had removed his liver for medical research, and had replaced it with the liver of a non-Jew. The yeshiva students were livid: their friend, Hirshel, had been buried with the organ of a non-Jew! Bristling with righteous indignation, the *bochurim* decided to climb over the cemetery wall in the dead of the night, dig up Hirshel's body, remove his liver, and rebury him. This was an extremely dangerous idea—especially in wartime.

Meanwhile, Reb Zavel Zeidenfeld, a *polisher* Chassid living in Rostov—having been forced to leave Poland during World War I—got wind of this risky plan. "Are you out of your mind?" he berated the *bochurim*. "You can't possibly do something this dangerous! As it is, the government is monitoring the Rebbe; if they find out what you have done, the Rebbe will feel the brunt of their fury."

Reb Zavel became so upset that he decided to enter the Rebbe's room and inform him of the situation. As soon as he finished speaking, the Rebbe made a dismissive gesture and said, "The liver of a *goy* is nothing, it is like dirt."

Reb Zavel was flabbergasted. The Rebbe, as a rule, spoke only Chassidus. He had never heard the Rebbe give a *halachic* ruling before!

Seeing his bewilderment, the Rebbe continued, "If you want, you can write to the Rogatchover *gaon* for his opinion."

Reb Zavel exited the Rebbe's room and told the *bochurim* what had transpired. They quickly sent a letter off to the Rogatchover; within a few days, a postcard arrived from the *gaon*. On the postcard, the *gaon* had written *exactly the same words* Reb Zavel had heard from the Rebbe, followed by a string of Torah sources! Everyone was taken aback at the clear proficiency of the Rebbe, even in an uncommon field of *halacha*.

Another short incident, but one with an important lesson to learn, occurred when *Zaidy* and his father were walking with a group of Chassidim, including the eminent Chassid Reb Peretz Motchkin, toward a *farbrengen*. Among the group were both younger *bochrim* and married Chassidim.

As the group made their way to the *farbrengen*, they came to a crossroads: the faster route passed a public swimming pool, while the longer route passed through a quiet, residential neighborhood. It was a hot day and some in the sweltering group voiced an opinion to take the shorter route and reach their destination faster. "But that's not right," Reb Peretz called out, "there are *bochurim* in this group! A public swimming pool is not a place for *bochurim* to be seen!"

Zaidy's father stopped in midstride. "I don't understand this," he said. "And for married people it *is* permissible to pass a not-*tzniyusdik* area, like a public swimming pool!?"

Embarrassed by the glaring truth of his statement, the group turned away from the shorter route and took the longer road to the *farbrengen*.

Another incident *Zaidy* often related was about a *farbrengen* that transpired in the difficult days following the departure of the Rebbe Rayatz from the Soviet Union. Although the Rebbe had assured his followers that their welfare would forever remain paramount in his mind, Chassidim were devastated to lose the physical proximity to their life—the Rebbe. Their feeling of dejection and isolation heightened as the Communists stepped up their religious oppression against the Chassidim—nary a week passed without news of another arrest, exile, or murder of a fellow Chassid.

With this background in mind, it becomes easier to understand how Chassidim found it difficult to muster the energy to look ahead for brighter days, to find the inner strength to create a positive mood and sit together in warm comradery at a *farbrengen.*

And so, on *yud beis tammuz,* the newest celebratory day marked on the Chassidic calendar, *Zaidy*—still a young man— and friends attended a clandestine *farbrengen* in the home of Reb Zalman Kozliner, attended by some of the greatest Chassidim remaining in Russia, including Reb Bentzi Maroz, Berel Battumer, and Reb Nissen Nemanow. Later to influence thousands of students in Yeshivas Tomchei Tmimim of France, Reb Nissen distinguished himself with piety and abstinence, but his most acclaimed characteristic was *kabbolas ol,* the unquestioning commitment to every aspect of Chassidus—but even he could not find the ability to start speaking and get the *farbrengen* underway.

The clock ticked off minute by minute, but the *farbrengen* was not taking hold; nothing was happening. "It is infernally hot," one of the Chassidim said. "Can someone go and get us two quarts of *kvass* (a fizzy grain drink)."

Someone ran out to get two bottles of freezing cold *kvass,* handing the bottles to *Zaidy* when they returned. But *Zaidy,* intent on getting the *farbrengen* started, decided to secretly mix in some *mashke*. He poured a cup that was really two-thirds *kvass* and one-third *vodka* and gave the concoction to Reb Bentzi Maroz. "This tastes very good," said Reb Bentzi. "Get me another cup."

Feeling emboldened, this time *Zaidy* mixed in half a cup of *kvass* and half a cup of vodka. "*Nu*," said Reb Bentzi after downing his second cup of so-called *kvass*, "it's time we started *farbrenging*." He started singing a pensive *niggun*; slowly, surely, everyone else began singing along and the *farbrengen* progressed from that point on—well through the night.

Another short encounter with a famous personage, this time with Rabbi J. B. Soloveitchik, occurred many, many years later:

After *Zaidy* arrived in New York, he began working as a *shochet* for a Brooklyn meat plant operated by Swift & Co. The owner of the plant, acutely aware of the peculiar nature of kosher beef, had made a name for himself by buying and distributing the cuts of meat prized by New York's exclusive restaurants; soon the company was selling all over the United States, becoming the nation's largest kosher beef wholesaler.

Although the owner was a Reform Jew, he was adept at pro-visioning *glatt shechita* for his Chassidic and Orthodox cus-tomers, a demanding standard that other slaughterhouse owners had a hard time understanding.

Committed to respecting the preferences of others, the owner worked diligently to make sure his plant met the requirements of the supervising *rabbonim*.

One of these *rabbonim* was the famous Rabbi Joseph B. Soloveitchik, scion of the Lithuanian Jewish Soloveitchik rabbinic dynasty. His grandfather, the famous "Reb Chaim Brisker," served as *rosh yeshiva* of the Volozhiner Yeshiva for many years and became famous for formulating his "Brisker method" that stresses precise definitions of the *gemara* with particular emphasis on the Rambam.

Rabbi Soloveitchik once came to the slaughterhouse while *Zaidy* was standing in the *shechita* line. Standing next to him was a *talmid* of the *mussar* movement of Novardok, and the *Rav* came over to their area as part of his *kashrus* inspection.

"Can I ask the *Rav* a question?" the Novardoker asked.

"Yes."

"People always talk about the great Yeshiva of Volozyhn," said the Novardoker. "Why, in the Volozhyn of old, didn't they allow the students to learn *Mussar?*"

The *Rav* turned to him and asked loudly: "I have a far greater question—why did they not institute a set time every day in Yeshivas Volozyhn for the students to learn Chassidus?"

Rabbi Soloveitchik emphasized this by exclaiming: "Do you know what Chassidus did? Chassidus revolutionized *Yiddishkeit!*"

That Rabbi Soloveitchik—teacher, writer, foremost Talmudist, and community leader who shaped Modern Jewry in America—would make such a public statement made a deep impression on all the people in the room. *Zaidy* was very taken by this short exchange and repeated it often.

Another fascinating personality *Zaidy* liked talking about was—Reb Yisrael Gottesman. Back in the 1940's, although not a Chabad *chassid*, Reb Yisrael would walk in from Williamsburg to Crown Heights every Shabbos that the Rebbe Rayatz would come out for a *farbrengen*. When the Rebbe's son-in-law and future Rebbe arrived in America, he was reluctant to say the word 'G-d' that appears in this Chassid's surname, preferring to call him by the name *Reb Yisrael Baal Shem* instead. The name stuck.

Once, as Reb Yisrael waited in line to enter the room of the Rebbe Rayatz for *yechidus*, the Rebbe's attendant came out and stopped the line. "The Rebbe is feeling unwell," he apologized.

Everyone left quietly—except for Reb Yisrael. He began pestering the attendant, insisting in the strongest terms that he *had to* consult with the Rebbe about a very urgent matter. "*Ich miz araingeyn!*" he demanded. The poor attendant became so flustered that he reentered the Rebbe's room, apologizing for the intrusion, and asked for instructions. "Let him in," said the Rebbe Rayatz.

As soon as Reb Yisrael entered the room, he began showering the Rebbe with *brochos*: "*The Rebbe should be gezunt! Hashem should give the Rebbe strength! The Rebbe should merit to lead us toward Moshiach!*"

Reb Yisrael then ran out of the room and left the building.

The Rebbe immediately called in his attendant and said, "He enlivened me! Call everyone back; *yechidus* will resume."

Years later, when *Zaidy* arrived in America, he became friendly with this *Reb Yisrael Baal Shem* and often offered him to stay in his home after a *farbrengen*, instead of making the trek back to Williamsburg.

Once, *Zaidy* and a group of Chassidim asked Reb Yisrael, "Why do you walk in from Williamsburg just to hear the *farbrengens* when you are not even a Lubavitcher?"

"Have you ever thought what our Sages meant when they said, *Tzaddikim create peace in the world?*" Reb Yisrael said animatedly. "When a baby cries, what do you do? You give the baby a bottle. The same is true of the Jewish people: when they need Divine assistance they approach the *tzaddik* and he is their "bottle," creating peace.

"But what happens when you don't have a bottle ready? How do you soothe the crying infant? You take an empty bottle and stick it in the baby's mouth, hoping for a few minutes of quiet until you can get a real bottle ready. The baby begins sucking on the nipple until, after a few minutes, he realizes nothing is in the bottle, spits it out, and resumes crying. At this point, you have no choice but to put the empty bottle back in again for another few minutes of quiet until the baby realizes and starts crying—and the cycle resumes again.

"Listen to me," concluded Reb Yisrael. "All the other Rebbeim are 'empty bottles,' but the Lubavitcher Rebbe is full of milk; he satiates his Chassidim. And that is why I walk in from Williamsburg."

TRUTH REVEALED

"And Yitzchak, experiencing a great dread, shuddered in bewilderment..." (Toldos, 27:33)

Why was Yitzchak so frightened? What new piece of information caused him to become so confused?

Yitzchak knew very well that Yakov was a good and studious child, while Eisav was the troublemaker. Yet, when the time came to bestow such powerful Divine blessings—blessings that granted the recipient both the abundance of Heaven and dominion over other Nations—he felt that Yakov was too mild mannered and simple to know what to do with such blessings. Eisav, on the other hand, was a 'chevreman'—although he was a scamp.

Therefore, Yitzchak intended to bestow the blessings on Eisav.

But now, as Yitzchak realized the deception played by his "mild mannered" son, he realized that Yakov was the true 'chevreman!' This son would truly know what to do with such awe-inspiring blessings! This completely reversed his entire mode of thinking, causing Yitzchok to be greatly afraid—he had com-

pletely underestimated his younger son!—and leading him to exclaim, "Who is he who came to me with food? He will indeed be blessed."

When Eisav immediately followed up by telling his father that this was Yakov's second (!) deception—having already deprived Eisav of the birthright—this further enforced Yitzchak's realization that Yakov was, in fact, the real 'chevreman' in the family ...

—Zaidy

CIRCLE OF MELODY

Anyone attending *Zaidy's farbrengens* quickly realized that singing *niggunim* was a central part of the way *Zaidy* transmitted the Chassidic flavor of yesteryear. Better said, singing *niggunim* was a central part of his life.

This fascination with *niggunim* began even in *Zaidy's* younger years. He enjoyed telling the story of how his phenomenal recollection of *niggunim* stayed with him throughout the travails of his turbulent life, even trumping the recollections of others perhaps more musically inclined.

The short story Zaidy enjoyed telling—one that had an interesting outcome many years later—involved a chance meeting on the train between himself and Reb Moshe Charitonow, a brother of the famous Chabad composer, Reb Aharon Charitonow. Zaidy had a remarkable ear for music and, when he saw the brother of the celebrated baal menagen, he went over and in-

troduced himself. "Listen," said Reb Moshe. "There's a new *niggun* my brother, Sholom, recently composed; I want to teach it to you."

And so, as the train clattered its way across the railroad, the eminent Reb Moshe Charitonow taught a new Chabad *niggun* to a young child.

Many decades later, in New York, the Rebbe established *Nichoach*—an organization that produced authentic recordings of Chabad *niggunim*, exactly the way they were sung throughout generations. These included the atmospheric melodies that mark Chassidic occasions, Shabbos, and Yom Tov.

At one point, when the Rebbe suggested to the organizers to contact elder Chassidim in the hope of recording more *niggunim*, one of the organizers paid *Zaidy* a visit, asking if he perhaps had something new to offer. "Yes!" *Zaidy* said, "I once met Reb Moshe Charitonow on the train and he taught me a new *niggun* composed by his brother, Aharon."

Zaidy then proceeded to teach them the *niggun* he had heard so many years earlier—a stately tune similar to a Chassidic waltz. *Zaidy* also taught them the correct way to sing the *niggun* attributed to his father, Reb Chonye. The organizers at *Nichoach* decided to release both tunes back-to-back on the same recording.

When *Nichoach* #13 was released, the Charitonow family was taken aback to find a melody attributed to their father— one completely unknown to them! Reading the acknowledgments on the jacket cover, they found *Zaidy's* name, and they approached him for clarification. "Our father never composed such a *niggun*!" they protested. "The setting is completely different than his usual style! You must have imagined it or heard it from someone else."

Never one to back down, *Zaidy* remained insistent that he had heard this melody *just so* from their uncle; the family, for their part, were insistent that the melody had been taken from a different composer. Some time passed. One day, *Zaidy* received a call: the Charitonow family had been sorting through voluminous piles of sheet music left behind by Reb Aharon when, to their immense surprise, they found the *niggun Zaidy* had been singing all along! (Whenever *Zaidy* told this story at *farbrengen*, we all knew he would insist on singing that particular *niggun* next ...)

Zaidy often related the story of how his father, on a visit to Rostov, had the immense *zechus* to have the Rebbe Rashab personally teach him all ten *niggunim* traditionally composed by the Alter Rebbe. *Zaidy's* father had a deep appreciation for music and a smooth singing voice.

Years later, after the Rebbe Rayatz had escaped Russia and was living temporarily in Poland, he wrote to *Zaidy's* father, asking him to get all ten *niggunim* recorded in musical notes and to send them to him. This was not as simple as it sounds: *Niggunim*, transmitted orally through the generations, invariably suffer unintentional changes along the way. A variation or two is bound to creep in somewhere. To set these *niggunim* to precise musical notes would be a difficult undertaking.

Reb Chonye searched until he found an elderly *chazzan*, to whom he sang every movement of each *niggun*. The chazzan transcribed the musical notes and, after every *niggun*, *Zaidy's* father asked the *chazzan* to sing the melody back from the newly transcribed notes. Although the notes were transcribed correctly, Reb Chonye could not help but sigh as the *chazzan* sang. "You sing it correctly," he muttered, "but the soul is missing from your singing!"

"What can I do?" the *chazzan* shrugged. "Musical notes cannot convey spiritual depth."

When the Rebbe received the musical sheets, he decided to publish these notes in *Hatomim*, a periodical published by Tomchei Tmimim in Otwock, Poland. He sent the editorial board a letter: "Reb Chonye has the unique advantage of having had my saintly father teach him the ten *niggunim* of the Alter Rebbe. Additionally, he knows the musical movements and *niggunim* which my saintly father used when he sang during his prayers on weekdays and *Shabbos*. The editors should find a competent musician to transcribe those musical movements as well." (Only one of these transcripts saw publication before the Nazis invaded Poland.)

Zaidy heard all these ten *niggunim* from his father, who often sang them at *farbrengens* he led, indicating which ones the Rebbe Rashab used when he sang during his *davening*. "When he sang the tune to *Likras Shabbos* on Friday nights," said Reb Chonye, "the Rebbe *always* sighed after singing 'Hashem is One.' That sigh is impossible to replicate."

From the ten *niggunim*, seven attained popularity—sung at *farbrengens*, taught in schools, hummed during *davening*. It would not be an exaggeration to say that *Zaidy* felt it his "duty"—as practically the only one still alive who could impart these *niggunim* in America—to transmit the other three *niggunim* to as many people as possible.

Thus, whenever *Zaidy* began telling this abovementioned story of the *niggunim*, the younger crowd at the *farbrengen* usually broke out in muffled, good-natured groans: They knew that *Zaidy* would now spend a half hour or so teaching these three *niggunim* again, sometimes with tears streaming down his face, and nothing could distract him until he finished singing all three *niggunim*.

It remains entirely to his unwavering dedication to transmit the golden chain of the Alter Rebbe's *niggunim*, that, today, thousands of Chassidim all across the globe are familiar with these *niggunim*.

INTELLECTUAL PERIL

"If the daughter of a Kohen defiles herself by starting to pursue adultery (Vayikra 21:9)"

"Chassidus teaches that souls are called "the daughter of a Kohen" since 'Kohen' alludes to chessed, the manifestation of Divine loving kindness.

"The verse uses the Hebrew word 'Saychel.' By using a play on the word–using its parallel in Yiddish–the same word ('Saychel') means 'intellect.'

"Humans were granted a superior level of intellect, but precisely this superiority comes with inherent pitfalls–and can lead a person to stray from their purpose and behave even worse than animals.

"Sometimes, we can become deluded, thinking we have reached the level of a 'Kohen'–one who is completely attuned to spirituality–and we forget how fragile and susceptible to sin we really are. With this interpretation in mind, the verse now reads–

"A soul that thinks it is as spiritual as a Kohen can be led astray by its intellect, and become defiled."

"History is littered with people who, thinking they were

'Kohanim,' became complacent and allowed themselves to be led astray by all sorts of philosophical justifications. The only way to stay focused on the straight and narrow is through humility.

–Zaidy

JOURNEYS

Sometimes—usually in the setting of a quieter, intimate *farbrengen*—*Zaidy* related a frightening incident that occurred while the Marosow family still lived in Leningrad.

This was well after the age of the *Enlightenment*—whose followers wrote poems and plays in Yiddish, replete with humorous jibes at rabbis and Jewish leaders, making the ridicule Torah and its *mitzvos* an acceptable practice. The movement had already wreaked spiritual havoc throughout Jewish Germany and now its influence began spreading throughout Russia and the Ukraine, spinning a web across the strata of Jewish communal life. Many impressionable young minds, led astray by secular books containing heretical ideas, were casting away their heritage, preferring to live like secular gentiles.

In Leningrad, too, many young Jews were indistinguishable from the gentile neighbors. It thus occurred that, on the ground floor of the residential building where the Marosow's lived, stood an apartment occupied by two Jewish girls—Jewish in name alone. They lived with gentile boys and acted completely indifferent to their heritage—they even wore a large cross around their necks. *Zaidy's* parents and siblings avoided eye contact with these girls whenever their paths crossed; they simply could not acknowledge the sacrilegious lifestyle of these people. Religious Jews would spit in the direction of this ground floor apartment.

Meanwhile, still smarting from their defeat in World War I, many Russians began venting their patriotic rage on the hapless Jews, and, one Sunday, the local priest stirred his congregation into a frenzy of religious anger, exhorting them to take revenge on the Jews for the sake of Mother Russia. Soon a mob of angry, shouting madmen intent on killing Jews began making a beeline—for *Zaidy's* building. The Marosow family and all the other Jewish neighbors watched in terror from behind their curtained windows; all avenues of escape were closed off, they faced a certain death.

The mob shattered the front door and spilled into the lobby, stopping up short when two smartly dressed women emerged from their ground floor apartment, crosses dangling from their necks. "Dear ladies," smiled the priest, "show us where the Jews live in this building."

"Jews?" replied the women. "What are you talking about? There are no Jews in this building! We swear on the cross."

Apologizing profusely, the priest turned to the mob and ordered them out of the building and toward their next target.

Zaidy felt an entirely different respect for these people from then on. "This incident taught me not to judge a Jew's true worth based on their external appearance," he explained. "There was a very real chance that someone would have recognized the women as being Jewish themselves; they would have been killed instantly and the building thoroughly searched—but they did not hesitate in the slightest to lie about their identity and the Jews living in the building. The hard truth is that, had these women not intervened, I would not be alive today. They saved all the Jews living in our building; no one ever spat in the direction of their apartment ever again."

(To illustrate the difficulties entailed in staying a practicing Jew in Soviet Russia, *Zaidy* sometimes told the story of Reb Binyamin Ramano, who stayed a Chassid because of the Communists! This Reb Binyamin decided he could no longer live with the ongoing religious harassment against himself and his family, so he decided to become a card carrying Communist instead.

He married a non-Jewish wife. He discarded his Jewish attire and off he went to the local Communist branch. He was greeted with a barrage of questions as the Communists probed his reasons for leaving *Yiddishkeit*. "I'll tell you the truth," he finally said. "I don't believe in your ideology at all; it's just that I can't get any benefits from being a religious Jew—I won't get housing, employment, or food from the Jews. But I will get it all if I become a Communist."

His Communist interrogators were less than impressed. "So, if the time comes and Communism is not able to provide these basic comforts for you—you will then say the same thing about us and leave the Communist party?" they asked.

"Yes," Reb Binyamin answered.

The Communists summarily threw him out of the office and refused his admission to the party. Embarrassed beyond belief, he divorced his wife, became a *baal* teshuva, and remained a practicing Jew.)

Zaidy was twenty years old when agents of the secret

police came to arrest his father. Reb Chonye had been hiding in the home of the Raskins with one of his young sons— hoping to evade arrest—but the KGB had tracked him down. "Let's take the boy with us as well and throw him into an orphanage," the agents said to one another. "He has no one to watch him.

The Jacobson children took heart and spoke up. "Leave him with us," they said bravely, "we will treat him like one of our own."

The agents gave the children a dubious look, but they left the boy alone, throwing Reb Chonye into an awaiting vehicle. *Zaidy* happened to be outside at the time and he quickly ran home to warn everyone. Reb Chonye was never seen again.

Bereft of her husband, *Zaidy's* mother moved the entire family to Moscow, hoping against hope they could find improved living conditions in a different city, but, as Germans advanced toward Moscow, *Zaidy* and his mother began discussing their next move.

Zaidy and his fellow Chassidim were euphoric about the advancing German army. In their minds, having suffered brutally under the brutal religious oppression of the Soviets, they could not imagine the Germans being any worse than the Soviets who had murdered both *Zaidy's* and *Bubby's* father. After all, the Germans were genteel and civilized. In this sense, their naiveté was mindboggling. The Soviet media did not report on any of the German atrocities, so that Russian Jews were generally unaware of the mass genocide being perpetrated across the border.

Zaidy's mother, however, felt a sense of unease about

staying in Moscow, and adamantly refused to continue living there. "Many of my friends have escaped to the safety of Tashkent," she told *Zaidy*. "We must escape."

(After the Bolsheviks removed the last emir from office in 1920, Bukhara maintained relative autonomy for a few years. At that point, it became part of the Soviet Republic of Uzbekistan. Tashkent developed into a major city, with Samarkand not far behind. The Soviets began settling Jewish workers on farms, establishing Jewish collective farms—*kolkhozes*—in Uzbekistan.

The Bolsheviks looked favorably at the Jews of Bukhara. For a few years, it seemed that a dual policy existed: while religious Jews were being arrested and prosecuted for practicing *Yiddishkeit* in the heart of Russia, Bukharian Jewry enjoyed relative calm and religious freedom. This attitude of tolerance—coming at a time when religious repression was sweeping the Soviet Union—worked to create an enclave of religious tolerance that defied logic. Jews in Bukhara were able to learn Torah, keep mitzvos, attend *shul* and public religious functions—while, in the same country ruled by the same government, their fellow Jews were being incarcerated or killed for these selfsame actions.

This dual policy prompted some of the most prestigious and revered Chabad Chassidic families to flee Central Russia and relocate to the two cities of Tashkent and Samarkand. In the easy lifestyle we enjoy today, it is difficult to fathom the difficulty of such a step: leaving behind family, friends, and possessions for weeks of torturous travel to an unfamiliar region—just to secure a greater measure of religious freedom.)

She prevailed in the end; *Zaidy* joined his family in the arduous trip to Tashkent. It was there that he met his future wife, Rosa Shagalow, daughter of the last *mohel* serving all the Jews of Homel; her father, too, had been murdered by the Soviets for helping other Jews fulfill the mitzvah of *bris milah.*

The young couple did not have a set of parents to walk them down to the *chuppa*, so Reb Nissan Nemanow and his wife and Reb Chaikel Chanin and his wife stood in as *unterfihrer*, escorting the bride and groom to the *chuppa*.

The young couple settled down in Tashkent for a few years. In 1946, after the end of World War II, they left Tashkent in a modern express train towards Lemberg, hoping to join fellow Chassidim fleeing the country under the false identities of Polish citizens returning to their homeland.

But now a new crisis threatened their escape: their newborn son did not yet have identification papers. Traveling without proper identification in postwar Russia had the potential of creating severe complications and almost certain arrest, but *Zaidy* put his trust in Hashem and the couple traveled out of Bukhara, praying fervently that no official would demand to see their paperwork.

Their newborn son, who was too young to eat solids, suffered terribly on the journey. There was nowhere they could warm up some water for the baby, nor was there any food they could give him, and the baby became very sick. By the time they reached Lemberg, the baby was so malnourished that they were forced to hospitalize him. The baby spent two weeks in the emergency ward, as doctors slowly, surely, built up his strength and saved him from certain death.

Meanwhile, during these two weeks, all other Chassidim in the group—including *Zaidy's* mother and siblings—traveled on to Lodz, their last stop before the border.

As soon as the baby began putting on weight, *Zaidy* traveled with his family to Lodz; there they met *Zaidy's* mother and siblings again. They stayed in Lodz for a few months. Reb Yakov Moshe Friedman had a house with four rooms; he installed dividers in each room and almost a dozen families found lodging there, sleeping at night on the floors.

From Lodz, the group traveled closer to the border, taking up residence in a border town. *Zaidy* and his family tried crossing the border twice—a distance of twenty kilometers. They would set out at night, carrying nothing but their infant son and a few necessities for the baby, hoping and praying not to be caught. Their first attempt ended in failure: as they neared the border, the crossing guards spotted them and ordered them back onto Russian soil. The second time they attempted to cross the border, they heard the stuttering sound of gunfire, and the group quickly retraced their steps.

The third crossing began under very difficult circumstances. A soaking rain began falling; when *Zaidy* went outdoors, he realized with a sinking heart that he could not take his infant son in such weather. In the end, this soaking downpour served as the perfect cover for *everyone else* to escape—after successfully crossing the border, they were taken by train and housed temporarily in the DP camps stationed in Poking. But *Zaidy* and his family were stranded; there was a real possibility they would remain behind in Russia.

After many obstacles, they finally made it over the border, into Germany. Meanwhile, the Allies had emptied out the city of Schwabhausen, transferring the homes instead to the war refugees; they did this with a vengeance against the Germans. *Zaidy* lived there for over a year, until finally their visas arrived allowing them entry into France.

They spent four years in Paris, France until, in 1950, an interesting train of events brought them to—Ireland. At first, *Zaidy* traveled there alone for a few months, sending for his wife and children later. They lived in Ireland for two years.

Just mentioning the word "Ireland" evokes a landscape varied by sweeping vistas and tranquil lakes, striking seashores, and emerald-hued grasslands. Throwing in a handful of bearded Chassidim threatens to skew the aesthetics of that landscape—but that is exactly what happened to *Zaidy* and his fellow Chassidim.

After the liberation, Jewish families living in DP camps were horrified and outraged to learn that non-Kosher meat was being sent to the DP camps, and they threatened to burn down the kosher kitchens operating in the camps. In an attempt to convince the Jewish agencies to provide Kosher meat, a letter was written to the Rebbe Rayatz in America who, in turn, penned a sharp letter to the agencies involved. These agencies then turned their attention to finding a viable and reliable source of Kosher food. One of these sources came from Ireland, a land where lush pastures create perfect breeding grounds for raising cattle.

The Irish government went so far as to offer one million pounds of kosher meat for the DP camps—part of a larger relief package of ten million pounds of meat donated for general relief purposes in Europe. This venture became known as the "Irish Meat Project."

The kosher meat aspect of the project was run under Mr. Robert Briscoe, an Irish-Jewish member of parliament. He flew to Paris to meet with the agencies involved, informing them that Chief Rabbi Herzog did not accept the worthiness of the *shochatim* currently serving in Ireland. "Therefore," he suggested, "we plan to employ Chabad *shochatim* and *mashgichim* from Germany and Russia."

This project created jobs for many Chabad Chassidim who moved to Ireland to *shecht* for the Jews in Europe. Logistics for the move was facilitated by Rabbi Binyomin Gorodetsky, who served as the personal representative of the Rebbe to coordinate the refugee work in Europe. The first group of Chabad Chassidim to arrive in Ireland was comprised of some of the most illustrious Chabad families.

Zaidy and his family—they already had four children— were part of the group that arrived in the early 1950's. Although the "Irish Meat Project" had ended, their execution and production of Kosher meat was such a resounding success that the agencies decided to duplicate the project to help provide the fledgling State of Israel with meat for her citizens. In addition, Mr. Briscoe decided to turn his past successes into a private business venture—necessitating even more *shochatim*.

Having Chassidim of such stature live, learn, *daven*, and work in Dublin made a tremendous impact on the local Jewish community. Already during the first Tishrei after their arrival, Mr. Briscoe had jumped up to the *bima* on Simchas Torah and announced, "Until these Chassidim came, we were practicing Jews, but we did everything by rote. Our observances were lackluster, robotic. These Chassidim have granted us a 'breath of life!' Just see how our lives have been affected by their joy and enthusiasm. Jews of Dublin! Jews like these are crucial for our survival; they have completely revitalized our community."

Zaidy sometimes related two anecdotes about his time in Ireland. These all occurred in the early 1950's, after the passing of the Rebbe Rayatz, and the succession of the Rebbe:

There was a group that met every day to learn a folio or two of *gemara* in Dublin's local *shul.* They called themselves the "*Chevra Shas.*" The *shiur* was led by a handful of teachers—Chassidim and non-Chassidim alike—but, if a visiting scholar came to town, they gave him the honor of giving the *shiur.*

At the time of the incident, a distinguished figure had arrived to visit his fellow Chassidim residing temporarily in Ireland. This was none other than Reb Bentzion ('Bentche') Shemtov. The Rebbe's brother had suddenly died in Liverpool, England and he had dispatched Reb Bentche to deal with the funeral arrangements and ensure the burial take place in Tzfas, Israel. Reb Bentche was well known to his fellow Chassidim for his complete and absolute self-negation and deep commitment to the Rebbe. For example, Reb Bentche never sat in the presence of the Rebbe; he only stood.

On the day he visited, another distinguished and unknown personage appeared in the *shul* and, after a hurried consultation, those attending the daily *shiur* decided to give him the honor of teaching that day's *gemara.* The group sat down around a table in *shul,* opening up to the last folio in *Meseches Kesuvos.* Reb Bentche sat down near *Zaidy.* The visiting rabbi taught the *gemara* and *rashi* and then began explaining the *tosafos* on the margins of the page.

At one point, as the visitor was explaining the *tosafos,* *Zaidy* spoke up and pointed out a mistake in his interpretation, and corrected the mistake. When the visitor insisted his interpretation was correct, *Zaidy* posed a thorny question.

The teacher fell silent. He started thinking, beads of perspiration appearing on his forehead. The *shul* was quiet; all one could hear was the ticking of the clock on the *shul* wall. But then *Zaidy* felt someone shaking next to him. He turned around and saw Reb Bentche vibrating with silent laughter, his face radiant with admiration.

"You ask well," said the guest teacher finally. "I will think about it and send you a letter with the reply when I return home to Gateshead." He then closed the *gemara,* indicating the *shiur* had ended, and left the *shul.*

Gateshead! *Zaidy* had no idea the visitor was from Gateshead. "Marosow, what did you do?" one of the community members elbowed him. "You know who that was? You just stood up to the Gateshead *rosh yeshiva!*"

"Well done!" interrupted Reb Bentche. "I live in England and I know who that was. You made a tremendous *kiddush shem Lubavitch.* Until now, that *rosh yeshiva* was under the impression that Chassidim cannot learn *gemara;* thanks to you, he now knows the truth about Chassidim and about Lubavitch."

(Whenever he related this story, *Zaidy* would end off by saying, "I'm still waiting to get that letter from the Gateshead *rosh yeshiva* with the answer to my question!" This usually prompted gales of laughter from people at the *farbrengen*.)

Very rarely—as though he felt somewhat embarrassed by his presumptiveness in overturning the staid atmosphere of the *shul* in Dublin—*Zaidy* would retell the "*Incident with the Maggid*."

One summer day, *Zaidy* sat in *shul* learning with the congregants of the Dublin *kehilla*, and some fellow Chassidim who were also working as *shochtim*. The door opened and a traveling Maggid walked in. Back in Europe, these Maggidim were celebrated and adored by congregations who crowded synagogues to hear them preach. Many of these were *Mussar* preachers who focused entirely on sin and repentance, usually degrading the innate worth of the Jewish people and raising the audience to a high pitch of religious fervor.

Many of the wandering Maggidim acted also as charity collectors—soliciting for themselves as well as charitable institutions abroad—and this Maggid would also be collecting money from the congregation for his speech.

Stories abound of the Baal Shem Tov clashing with Maggidim, strongly denouncing the way they denigrated the Torah study and mitzvah observance of simple Jews, and these stories flashed through *Zaidy's* mind as the Maggid asked permission to address the *shul* until *Mincha*. Permission was granted, everyone closed their *sefarim*, and the congregation settled down to listen to the Maggid.

It was a hot summer day; a sultry breeze blew in through the synagogue windows, and everyone sat quietly in their shirtsleeves. The Maggid, an older person with a silver tongue, began speaking about certain stories of the *Avos* and of Yosef and his brothers, and, at a certain point, spoke about the *Avos* in a very crude and disrespectful way, finding fault with their conduct.

Zaidy was horrified. As explained in *Tanya*, the Patriarchs are compared to the *merkava*, the spiritual chariot of Hashem, and were conduits to spiritual light, drawing lofty levels of Divinity into this world—yet here the Maggid was describing them as simpletons with boorish mannerisms. *Zaidy* became so infuriated that he jumped out of his seat, ran over to the *bima*, and began banging loudly on the lectern, announcing, "*Mincha! Mincha!*"

The *shul* erupted. Some congregants immediately got up and began getting ready for *Mincha*; others wanted to know whether the Maggid had finished his speech; others professed shock at *Zaidy* for disturbing the *shul's* atmosphere with his shouting—there was a lot of finger pointing and arguing. The Maggid, for his part, slunk out of the *shul* and never returned.

Zaidy and the other *shochatim* were dealt a blow when Mr. Briscoe's enterprises began failing; he folded the enterprise practically overnight and they all traveled back to Paris. From there, they would eventually depart for American shores.

TIKKUN

Our Sages tell us (Brochos, 26b) that Avraham tikain Shacharis...."–

Avraham instituted Shacharis.

Yitzchak instituted Mincha.

Yakov instituted Maariv.

And what did Noach do? Nothing? Noach did not have the greatness to institute an everlasting tikkun?

But the truth is that Noach instituted a great tikkun:

Noach was the first person to develop alcoholic beverages, which "gladdens the heart of Hashem and of man (Shoftim, 9:13)."

Thanks to Noach, Jews throughout history have been able

to pour each other a shot of l'chayim and wish each other blessings.

–Zaidy, in jest

ADDENDUM

THE PHOTO

Zaidy had the incredible fortune of growing up in the presence of the Rebbe Rayatz. At times, he literally saw the Rayatz on a daily basis. As such, *Zaidy's* recollection of the Rebbe's physical appearance was based on how the Rebbe appeared prior to his arrest by the Soviets.

After the Communists announced their intention to abolish all religious privileges—including the strict ban against religious practices—rabbis, *mohalim*, and *shochtim* were summarily arrested, tried, and exiled—many never to return. Some, like *Zaidy's* father, were immediately murdered in cold blood.

Tragically, the actual assault on Jewish life came from the *yevsektzia*—Jewish members of the Communist Party. They fought fellow Jews with great fervor, closing synagogues and schools, banning *shechita* and *milah*, closing *mikvaos*. The *yevsektzia* became increasingly brutal, telling their non-Jewish counterparts that only the *yevsektzia*, as former Jews themselves, could successfully eradicate every trace of religious Jewish life. *Yiddishkeit* effectively went underground.

It was against this backdrop of religious persecution that the Rebbe Rayatz began his superhuman efforts in keeping the spark of *Yiddishkeit* alive—no matter the price in blood and tears. The Rebbe summoned a select few to join in this dangerous struggle, making a dramatic pact with nine select Chassidim—effectively forming a *minyan*—to continue these efforts under all circumstances, even to their "last drop of blood." Tragically, these words turned out to be prophetic: almost all members of this group met an untimely end, murdered in cold blood by the Soviets for their association with the Rebbe.

Zaidy's father was one of those select few.

Meanwhile, events were quickly spiraling toward a dangerous confrontation with the Soviets. Already back in 1920, *yevsektzia* agents began monitoring the Rebbe Rayatz in Rostov. When the Rebbe moved to Leningrad, the government assumed the Rebbe would curtail his religious efforts in such a central location, but they could not have been more wrong.

Matters came to a head in 1927. The *yevsektzia* decided they could no longer ignore the Rebbe's activities and began building a strong case of incriminating evidence against him. Not only did this knowledge not frighten the Rebbe, he publicly condemned his adversaries in public talks of Purim that year, frightening Chassidim with his impassioned words and blazing fervor.

On Tuesday night, the 14th of Sivan, 1927, the doorbell to the Rebbe's home pealed loudly, startling its inhabitants. A midnight ring could mean only one thing: the dreaded *yevsektzia*. Two agents burst into the house, a contingent of armed men following them inside. After confronting the Rebbe and his family, they began a thorough search of his house, arrested the Rebbe, and escorted him to a vehicle waiting to take him to the notorious Spalerka prison.

Jews throughout Russia and abroad were dumbfounded to hear of the Rebbe's arrest. No one had *really* believed the Soviets would dare lay a hand on an internationally known religious figure of such repute. Telegrams filled with outrage and protest flooded the Kremlin.

Meanwhile, in the dreaded Spalerka, the Rebbe was interrogated and tortured; some of the savage beatings he received were so damaging that he suffered impairment for the rest of his life. Seeing they would never succeed in intimidating the Rebbe, his sentence was reduced to three years exile to the city of Kostroma—deep inside Russia, far away from his Chassidim.

Less than two weeks later, as the Rebbe appeared at his obligatory appearance at police headquarters in Kostroma, the official behind the desk genially informed the Rebbe that he was free. However, with the specter of re-arrest hanging over his head, the Rebbe moved to Riga, Latvia. The news hit Chassidim very hard, knowing full well that they would never see their beloved Rebbe ever again.

Indeed, *Zaidy* never saw the Rebbe Rayatz again, only reaching the shores of America in 1953— three years after the Rebbe's *histalkus*.

Zaidy only remembered how the Rebbe looked prior to the torture and harassment in jail that had permanently altered his appearance. From then on, the Rebbe appeared prematurely aged; he did not stand with the same ramrod posture as before. Although he saw dozens of pictures taken during the time the Rebbe Rayatz lived in America, *Zaidy* could not fully relate to the Rebbe's appearance.

One day, in the 1990's, a treasure trove of previously unpublished photographs of the Rebbe Rayatz were publicized in a Chabad weekly magazine. Among the photos was a picture a much younger Rebbe Rayatz, standing tall and broad shouldered. When *Zaidy* saw this photo, he became extremely animated. "*This* is how I remember the Rebbe!" he kept repeating excitedly.

Zaidy went to a kitchen drawer, took out a pair of scissors, cut out the picture, and hung in the kitchen at eye level, so that he could see it every time he walked in and out of the room.

MIRACLE IN NUCLEAR CHERNOBYL

The meltdown at the Chernobyl Nuclear Power Plant in April of 1986 was a massive tragedy that ultimately claimed thousands of lives and affected millions. A toxic mess of radioactive particles choked the atmosphere and rained down on cities and forests. Tens of thousands were immediately evacuated. A direct consequence of Cold War isolation and lack of any safety culture, the nuclear explosion dominated international headlines for months.

The contaminated waste had to be buried deep underground, so the Soviet Union sent in humans—600,000 of them. Joining such a team was suicidal. These liquidators were charged with doing everything—from hosing down streets and homes to building concrete walls around the exposed reactor—while subatomic particles ravaged their cells and shortened their life spans. Workers were not provided with adequate protection and their direct contact with hazardous materials and the vapors they inhaled caused irreparable damage to their health, so that, in the years following the meltdown, thousands of these workers died from radiation-caused cancers.

Across the ocean, on a different continent, the phone rang in *Zaidy's* home. His wife, *Bubby* Rosa Marosow, an indefatigable worker for Friends of Refugees of Eastern Europe (F.R.E.E.), was a direct line of support for disoriented immigrants arriving from Russia. She found housing for them, furniture, jobs— everything they needed to start afresh in a new country— and a steady stream of people called to consult with her at all hours of the day.

Once these immigrants had regained a semblance of settled life, Bubby could now speak to them about enrolling their children in Jewish day schools, about attending *shul*, and about learning more about *Yiddishkeit.*

So, when the telephone rang late at night, everyone thought it was another newcomer from Russia in need of material support. Yet, this phone call was markedly different: the elderly couple on the phone wept as they spoke about their son, still residing in the Soviet Union, who had just receive orders to present himself and join a group slated to assist the nuclear reactor cleanup in Chernobyl. What could possibly be done to save their son from certain death?

Zaidy—listening on another extension—placated the couple. "There is a way," he said. "Give me your son's Hebrew name and all the information; I will write to the Rebbe immediately for his blessing." He jotted down all the details and composed a letter to the Rebbe, describing the terrible circumstances and asking for a *brocho.*

The Rebbe's blessing was not long in coming. The Rebbe *bentched* them for a positive outcome and blessed the son to be able to immigrate to America in the near future.

Time was running out for the young man. When the scheduled date arrived, he reported to the address as instructed, boarding one in a line of busses transporting hundreds of people to a location near the nuclear reactor zone. After a few hours, the busses pulled up outside a nondescript building. Scores of people waited nervously as an official with a megaphone began speaking. After expounding on the unique, patriotic privilege they shared for helping clean the contaminated areas, promising them a government pension, he started reading names off a clipboard, assigning people to their jobs.

The group thinned out as slowly, steadily, the crowd reboarded the buses for their final leg of the journey—the reactor. The courtyard was empty—*besides for this young man whose name had inexplicably not been called.* The young man loitered around the courtyard for a while, unsure of his next step; leaving without official permission could incur grave consequences. Finally, mustering his courage, he approached the official who was about to enter the building.

"No one called my name," he said. "May I go?"

The officer looked at him incredulously. "If no one called you," he said slowly, "that means they do not need you at the reactor. But you can't leave. Stay here; we need another clerk to help with the office work in this building."

The young man felt a surge of relief. He followed the officer into the building and immediately received a desk and an assignment, but there, from his office window he could still see the nuclear reactor site in the distance. Working in the building was safer than cleaning contaminants near the reactor—but not by much. He still felt a niggling sense of unease as he reported to work every morning.

One day, as he sat at his desk, the door to his office suddenly flew open and an unfamiliar officer walked in. "Give me your papers," he barked. "I will stamp them all and you are exempted from continuing; you can return home." The young man gave the officer his papers and watched, as though in a dream, as his papers were stamped and he was granted permission to return home. A short time later, he landed in New York, once again reunited with his parents.

A few weeks later, one of *Zaidy's* grandsons had an upcoming birthday and asked *Zaidy* to accompany him in the "Dollars line" before the Rebbe. At that time, the Rebbe was distributing dollars for *tzedaka* from his home, and they joined the long line snaking down President Street, waiting patiently under a sky swollen with gray clouds. Suddenly *Zaidy* noticed the distraught father who had called him about his son in Chernobyl, standing next to an unfamiliar young man. "This is my son!" the father said excitedly to *Zaidy*. "We came today to thank the Rebbe."

Sensing an opportunity, *Zaidy* and his grandson changed their place in the line to stand right behind the father and son. As they stood there in line, the son told *Zaidy* in detail everything that had transpired since that phone call and his miraculous escape from certain death.

Meanwhile, the line inched forward, moving up the front steps of the Rebbe's home to enter the front hall, then turning right into a brightly lit dining room area. At the far end stood the Rebbe, leaning slightly on a raised table, looking intently at every person who passed. Attendants pushed crisply minted dollar bills across the table. Now and then a flashbulb illuminated the scene. The line moved faster now—two people, then one, and then the father-and-son were standing in front of the Rebbe.

The older man was overcome with emotion. "Rebbe!" he said in Russian, "this is my son, the one you saved from Chernobyl. We came to thank you."

The Rebbe pointed upwards and replied, also in Russian, "Don't thank me; thank Hashem."

The older man remained undeterred. "We came to thank the Rebbe," he repeated.

Zaidy enjoyed telling this story at *farbrengens*, feeling privileged at having a "front row seat" to see these miraculous turn of events unfold.

POSTSCRIPT

Thirty years passed. People starting voicing questions and doubts about the veracity of the details in the story. After all, it sounded like something right out of the wonderworking stories found in *shivchi baal shem tov*—the last minute reprieve at the courtyard; the enigmatic savior in the office; the stunning turn of events that singled out one solitary survivor of this group of "liquidators." Were parts of the story embellished?

In 2016, word of this story reached the researchers at *My Encounter*, an oral history project geared at documenting the story of the Rebbe's life, and they became very keen in researching and interviewing the people involved in this story. They reached out to the Marosow's, asking them for contact information to reach this family, but the only phone number they could find was no longer in service. Their only lead had disappeared.

One day, a few months later, the father in the story passed away in his sleep. On his bedside table, in a sealed envelope, his son found a paper with the words "Call Mrs. Marasow when I pass away." The son immediately called, and she helped bring the departed father to *kever yisrael*. Armed with the updated phone number, the interviewing team at *My*

Encounter called to speak with the son. "I am very interested in meeting with you to tell my story," the son said, "but I am sitting *shiva* now. When the *shiva* is over, call me back to schedule an interview. I'm a doctor; so we can only meet at certain times when I'm not on call."

A few weeks later, a crew of audio and video technicians set out for the interview. The first thing they noticed upon entering the physician's home were the three large, framed portraits of the Rebbe gracing three rooms in the house.

And then, with the cameras rolling in the background, the physician sat down to relate the story of his "*Rescue at Nuclear Chernobyl*"—exactly the way *Zaidy* had been relating the story for years during his *farbrengens...*

Dedicated by
Leibi and Chanie Marozov

And their children Rivkah, Choni, Nosson Aaron, Maryasha

Dedicated by
**Rabbi Shmuel and Shaina
Lesches**

**And their children
Yosef, Schneur, Yocheved
Chaya, Mordechai**

Dedicated by
**Shmueli and Sora
Milecki**

**And their children
Chaya Kayla, Choni,
Ari, Ella Brocha**

Dedicated by

**Chony and Chanchie Milecki
And their children**

In Honor of our Parents
Rabbi Benzion and Henya Milecki
*Wishing you Nachas, Health, Hatzlacha, Nitzochon
and
Geulah!*

Dedicated by

Rabbi Shaya and Bayla Lesches

**And their children
Chana, Libah, Hadassa,
Mordechai, Chaya Mushka**

Dedicated by

Rabbi Chaim and Rivky Brikman

Dedicated by

**Rabbi and Mrs. Sender and
Chana Kavka**

**and their children
Menachem, Choni, Yeruchem, Yaakov**

לעילוי נשמת

הרב החסיד ר׳ מנחם מענדל
בן הרה״ח ר׳ אלחנן דוב ז״ל

מאראזאוו

יהי רצון שכל יוצאי חלציו יהיו כמותו

נדפס על ידי ולזכות נכדיו

יוחנן בן חנה וזוגתו דבורה לאה בת העניא נעומי
ומשפחתם

יוסף יצחק בן חנה וזוגתו שרה בת חיילה
ומשפחתם

יחיאל מיכל בן חנה וזוגתו שיינא עלקה בת
מרים ברײנדל
ומשפחתם

Made in the USA
Middletown, DE
27 November 2021